I0759436

MONK FRUIT

EDWARD SALEM

MONK FRUIT

NIGHTBOAT BOOKS
NEW YORK

Copyright © 2025 by Edward Salem

All rights reserved
Printed in the United States

ISBN: 978-1-64362-291-0

Design and composition by Kit Schluter
Typeset in Bembo Book MT Std

Cataloging-in-publication data is available
from the Library of Congress

Nightboat Books
New York
www.nightboat.org

for my father

CONTENTS

Elsewhere • 1
Monasticism • 2
Buddha's Bad Meal • 3
Whirling Dervish • 4
Secret • 5
Bleeding Tree • 6
Ode to ________ ________ • 9
Give What You Can • 10
Eat Cunt for Mental Health • 12
The Palestinian Chair • 13
Dabls • 15
Clit • 16
Why Stall • 20
Curb Your Enthusiasm • 21
David Schwimmer • 22
Misandry • 23
Aaron Bushnell Malachi Ritscher Mohamed Bouazizi • 24
Prop Comedian • 25
Pynchon • 26
Street Cats • 27
For Yara Flowers • 28
Septum • 30
Told You Obama Wouldn't Close Guantanamo • 31
Dunk Tank • 32
Kalthoum • 33
Hi, Mom! • 34
Tchotchke • 35
Osiris • 36
KSM • 37
Saint George Killing the Dragon • 38

Fasting for Gaza • 39
Go Left • 40
Promise of the Future • 42
Knowledge and Liberation • 43
Fullness • 44
Kalpas • 45
Hypnic Jerk • 46
Mao • 47
Tiger's Nest Monastery • 49
Fight • 51
Nose Kiss • 52
Jacuzzi • 53
Barbecue • 54
Infinity Is Just Another Place • 55
Pigeons • 56
The Sun's Silence • 58
Yogi • 59
Milieu • 60
At the Arab American National Museum • 61
L'Origine du Monde • 62
Landing in Israel • 63
Inside the Dome of the Rock • 64
Chaplin • 65
Determinism • 67
The Animal • 68
When I Died • 69
Species Dysphoria • 70
What a Light • 72
The Flea • 73
My Aerodynamics • 74
After Camões • 76
Final Montage • 77
Notes • 81
Acknowledgments • 83

Why don't you conceive of God as an ally who is coming . . .
the fruit of a tree whose leaves we are?
Why not project his birth into the future,
and live your life as an excruciating and lyrical moment
in the history of a prodigious pregnancy?

—RAINER MARIA RILKE

[The Absolute is] that moment in which something attains its maximum depth, its maximum reach, its maximum sense, and becomes completely uninteresting.

—JULIO CORTÁZAR

ELSEWHERE

I laughed at the phrase you used,
Emptied yourself. I thought,
It's true, there's nothing left.

I didn't remember how many
drinks I'd had as I poured another.
Who cares, I whispered to myself,

thinking back on our day together,
how glad I was
it was over—

earlier,
four men walking toward the border
were vaporized by a drone

that hovered haltingly
like a buzzing bumblebee
before the stigma of a flower.

MONASTICISM

Splotchy light warbles behind my eyelids.
I spit out each thought that tries to enter
like a wrinkled dollar rejected by a vending machine.

My eyes open to a tangle of power lines
drooping above Detroit backyards; a fruit fly
the color of the brown glass
of the beer bottle it's perched on.

BUDDHA'S BAD MEAL

Eating breakfast at the sunny bistro table, a bee landed in my orange juice
and swam desperately in circles around the glass, trying to free itself.
With cruel fascination, I watched this go on for some time.

The night before, I'd had a bad trip after taking too much of a psychedelic.
It built into a crushing, inescapable intensity. I woke my wife
and told her that the Big Bang was a cosmic suicide, the far future
an androgynous, universe-sized Christ who self-crucified
by exploding, which illuminated
the deeper meaning of the Palestinian suicide bomber.
She stifled laughter as she stroked my arm.

After a delicate sleep, I was able to stomach food.
Chatter from the souk below clotted the air.
The sky was an unblemished blue with a crystalline white sun.
The bee plopped into my glass of fresh-squeezed orange juice
and flailed, doggy-paddling not to drown, its wings submerged
as I watched it with my new knowledge
that there is no moral distinction between love and evil.

It wouldn't matter if I rescued the bee or let it drown.
Still, I tipped the glass and the juice rushed over the table,
the yellow in the orange squirming and blaring in the sun.

It crawled weakly off the balcony and fell over the ledge
down several stories onto the concrete below,
where it was trampled under tourists' feet.

WHIRLING DERVISH

I flirted with white lying that I was Muslim
for a chance at Riz Ahmed's $25,000 fellowship.
Maybe that doesn't count as a white lie.
But Sufism always spoke to me, even as a boy,
sneaking rum from my father's liquor cabinet
and pouring it into a can of lemon iced tea,
sprinting drunk till I collapsed on a sidewalk,
the suburban sky swirling, the black of my
closed eyes blasted with g-force.

SECRET

What is my body for?
In my youth I knew. I didn't
win the pull-up contest, but I won
the one where you hold yourself
above the bar, shaking so
your chin doesn't touch the metal.
I was in a sadomasochistic dynamic
with a friend my size,
our regular lunchtime game of
bloody knuckles turned into
a game of him punching me
as hard as he could, as many times
as we could secretly get away with,
in the back bleachers, in the chaos
of gym class, on my thigh and
upper arm, as I practiced
holding my face steady,
keeping my lips straight,
my voice held in, with each hit.
When I lifted my shirt or
shorts to show my friend
the dark purple swarming
my arms and legs, his eyes
widened and he laughed, not
a mocking laugh, but one of awe.
It made me happy to show him
the colors he made on me.
He admired my strength
more than his.

BLEEDING TREE

I have two therapists
who don't know about each other.
I've been seeing one for three years,
the other's brand new.
I see the old one monthly,
the new one weekly.
The old one's a Vienna-trained
Jungian analyst. The new one,
a less intellectual, soul-forward
"dynamical dialectic humanist"
drawing from mindfulness,
cognitive behavioral therapy,
and psychoanalysis. I do dream work
with the Jungian. I told him
I dreamt of Eddie Izzard
stepping on my balls,
toenails painted succulent red.
We talked about class and he told me
I'm part of the intelligentsia, implying
I'm better than the vacuous wealthy.
He said dictatorships first kill off
the intelligentsia, that's how prized,
how valuable I am.
I told the dynamical humanist I envied her
for valuing human connection above all else.
I'd rather have another zero
at the end of my paycheck
or a well-reviewed book, I said.
We talked about my father's poverty,

how he wiped his ass with stones,
shitting in a village field among other
dried human shit. Living in a house
with no plumbing or electricity,
no kitchen or bathroom.
A home improvement meant
carving a hole to squat over
behind the cement staircase.
The family ate meals by hand
sitting in a circle around firewood
in a windowless stone house built into a hill
so many grandfathers ago, no one
knows which ancestor built it.
I told her how I
suck down carbonated corn syrup,
ice cold, spiced and sweet,
while my father didn't drink ice water
till I don't know when.
We discussed class consciousness,
class complex, and she said, alternately,
classist, classicist, classism,
with an unsteadiness I read as unfamiliarity.

She's soul-forward, she makes me feel
heard and deeply understood,
whereas I often feel pressure to entertain,
to interest, my Jungian analyst.
I told him I dreamt of snapping twigs in two,
defecating in a peaceful squat.

Of a Cairene on the Nile
with a marigold neck tattoo
and a male-hating glare, capturing scarabs
and dressing them in bikinis.
Of crops irrigated with sewage water,
and wet mohawks shaped by praying hands.
I told him I dreamt that Buddha was a cow,
and Buddhism was an orange milk
that curdled and reeked as I drank.
I told him I dreamt of a bleeding tree.
Succulent red.

ODE TO ____________ ____________

Take off your pants as you read this,
push them down to your ankles.
Keep your underwear on,
don't be gross.

Open Instagram, close Instagram,
open Instagram, close Instagram
for two minutes straight,
which may feel absurd.

What are the odds you would've seen
slain Palestinians with your pants down
if you kept Instagram open?

Don't resent me for this
line of questioning.
This bearable conflation,
like magenta carnations
at the mass grave.

The action I'm asking
you to take
in this poem is. . .
you decide.
Just do something.
Assassinate Biden
's corpse.

GIVE WHAT YOU CAN

Hi, it's Bisan. I am still alive.
I'm sorry for the disturbing video.
There are no more universities.
No business as usual. No words.
Lavender. Coke. White phosphorus.
Come to Daddy. Finish the job. Give what you can.
All proceeds go to. The most moral army in the world.
Wiping out entire families from the public registry.
Mowing the lawn. Poppies. Child amputees.
Motaz. Plestia. Help us evacuate. Armed settlers.
Jewish Voice for Peace. Shaun King.
Ramy. Pinkwashing. Aaron Bushnell.
Red triangle. Red line.
Tatreez. Parachutes.
Losing your degree. From the river to the sea.
Helicopter lost in the mountains. No excuse
(to look away, deny or defend the 9enocide).
The second Nakba. The ongoing Nakba. Nakba 2.0.
If I Must Die. GoFundMe. The Pier.
Uncommitted. Art build. Hind Rajab. Tunnels.
Signal threads. Bird dogging. Kibbutz Blinken.
Refaat Alareer's Kite. Targeting journalists. Strawberries.
Hala Consulting and Tourism. Pepper spray. Aid trucks.
Sinwar's Stick. Drone strikes. Board of Regents.
US-made bombs. Marriage among tents.
Rashida Tlaib. Shadowbanned. Forced starvation.
Bella Hadid. Doxxed. Beheaded babies.
Never Biden. Student encampments. Fuck Bernie.
Fuck CNN. Diasporic Judaism. Internet outage.

@meta. Barricades. Jerusalem. Liberated zone.
Jennycide. Crossing into Egypt. Ceasefire Now.
$5,000 per adult. Watermelon. Atrocity fatigue.
H@mas. eSims. Khamas. Elbit Systems.
ICJ. PACBI. Zios. Teach in. Pariah state.
Instagram. Settler colonialism. Demolished hospitals.
Hind Hall. Court support needed.
Salaam Cola. Freedom flotilla. Resignations.
WAWOG. Hostage exchange. Car rally.
BDS. Return. Ismail Haniyeh.
IOF. Repost. Israhell. Naksa.
Palestinian Prison Literature. Velour blankets.
Movement lawyers. General strike. Satanyahu.
Anti-Zionist. General Assembly. Disrupting a weapons manufacturer.
Right to resist. Mutual aid. Ground operation.
Infants freeze to death. Normalization.
Apartheid. Western media. Manufactured famine.
Macklemore. Disappearing students.
Starbucks. Skunk water. Deported by ICE.
Globalize the intifada. Let Gaza Live.

EAT CUNT FOR MENTAL HEALTH

In the Lee Lozano monograph
on my coffee table, its cover
a crude drawing of a woman
with Stars of David for breasts,

a yellow page marker opens
to *Untitled (1961)*, her slogan
"EAT CUNT FOR MENTAL
HEALTH." I almost got it

tattooed in Arabic, but didn't
have her chutzpah—she boycotted
women for twenty plus years;
kept her ex-husband's last name,

and later, went by Leeeeeeeee,
then just E. In emails, I go,
Best,
E

THE PALESTINIAN CHAIR

God said (and already you can tell
I'm making this up),
If you lift a rock, I am there.
If you lift a finger, I am there.
If Blackwater rips out your fingernails,
I am there. God said,

If you're strapped into the contraption
the Israelis told the CIA they call
the Palestinian Chair,
hands tied to your ankles,
forcing you to lean forward in a crouch,
forcing all of your weight onto your thighs
as if you've been trapped in the act of kneeling
to pray, knees suspended above the floor,
arms pinned below your legs, blindfolded,
your head collapsed into your chest,
wheezing and gasping for air,
a pool of urine at your feet, too tired to cry,
but in too much pain to remain silent,
locked into a permanent squat
from which you can't recover,
I am there.

God said, when twenty million Yemenis
become silhouettes under pallid veils of skin
dying of starvation in 2016,
2020, 2024, 2028, 2032

while you scarf down lamb agdah
at Yemen Café in Hamtramck,
I am there.

After life is over,
you realize that

You were there.
For all of it.
It was all you.

DABLS

The African Bead Museum is falling apart.
A GoFundMe has been started.
There are already so many GoFundMes
going around. Lately life is like
six degrees of Kevin Bacon but instead
of Kevin Bacon it's Gazans fleeing 9enocide.
But Detroit has needs, too, I'm reminded,
or do I mean poor Black Americans who
once placed their Hope in Obama.
We're learning how to ride the internet
like an unbroken horse. We're giving money
to each other. $100, $25. Sometimes
a famous poet will give $500 and leave
their name up. The Dead Sea Scrolls
of the future could be screenshots
of a poet's donations or Gazan faces
or bejeweled, mirrored mosaics
falling from rotten cladding.

CLIT

1.

I saw *CLIT*
sprayed in fuzzy white
on the front door of a derelict house.

Tickled, I searched for
more of the artist's work
in the blighted recesses of the city.

Later, I found
a *CLIT* on another door
at the last house of a dead end

next to a highway,
but when I looked closer,
the L and I were joined,

forming a U—*CUT*—
which I learned meant
the utilities were cut off.

A message to squatters:
the crumbling, vacant home
has no electricity, heat or water,

so don't bother.
It's cold and
dark inside.

2.

The project house I bought
needed a new boiler, to begin with.
I spent the better part of that winter

stripping wallpaper, sanding floors,
hammering down bowing plaster,
slowly deciding to hire out the rest.

One night I found broken glass
and empty beer cans. I boarded
the window with plywood, but

a second window was shattered the next day.
In the half-demoed living room were scattered
cigarette butts and scraps of lettuce.

I waited in my car till she came back,
ranting belligerently, wearing three
baggy jackets and a faded black ballcap.

Mohammed! I don't fucking care,
Mohammed! she screamed down
the street when she saw me.

I gave her $250 to move on,
offered to drive her to a shelter,
call the United Way.

Walking away she waved

the wad of cash in the air,
shouting *Terrorist!*

It went on like this.
I installed a security system
and drove the heavy duffle bag

she left to a nearby church,
posted a note on my front door
saying where I'd taken it.

But she was waiting for me in the foyer,
duffle bag open, siren blaring,
ashing her cigarette on the floor.

3.

In the end only anger
persuaded her to leave
and never return.

Then contractors started work
and men were at the house
every day.

When it was time to paint
the new front door,
I spelled out *CLIT*

in long, free brushstrokes.
I took a picture with my phone
before painting it over.

WHY STALL

There's a docile fly in my bathroom
whose color seems off. Its husk is pallid
and plasticky like a tiny, winged designer
sneaker. I wave my hand before its eyes
but it doesn't move. Maybe the poor
guy's hungry, deep in dying stillness.

But what if instead,
it's an advanced drone made by DARPA
to surveil me in my bathroom?
Well, so what!

Privacy won't make the world
more known to itself, so why stall
the birth of God!

CURB YOUR ENTHUSIASM

Don't get too excited, in other words.
This isn't about the episode
"Palestinian Chicken."

It's about how Larry complained
(which is what every episode is about)
about how much time is wasted while urinating

and taped the "Gettysburg Address"
to the wall above the toilet to
memorize and make the time productive.

I find myself hovering my phone
before my torso while peeing
looking at

(insert genocidal image here).
I've saved the ones I haven't
memorized yet to my phone.

But I've memorized a lot of them.

DAVID SCHWIMMER

It's bitter consolation but—no matter
the jankiness of the comparisons—
most slaves weren't Frederick Douglass,
most whites weren't John Brown.

It took fifty years before
Friends' David Schwimmer
starred in the made-for-TV film
about the Warsaw ghetto uprising.

When will Palestinians get their own
David Schwimmer?

MISANDRY

It should go without saying
that all my sympathies lie
with the Seminole, Iroquois,
Ojibwe, etc. But I fear Palestinians,
like them, will fade from view.
The Hmong have, the Uyghurs,
the Rohingya. Black women
writing online, openly misandrist,
I envy them. I understand.
When white men fade away
in the far future, still then,
there won't be justice.
Just new people with
a short memory.

AARON BUSHNELL MALACHI RITSCHER MOHAMED BOUAZIZI

I wouldn't want to make a pariah of the executor
of my Last Will, but it'd be a riot to tie my corpse
to a bungee cord and affix it to a construction crane
where it would swing wildly above a parking lot,
splattering the pavement with embalming fluid

from on high. It would splash the front pages
of La Nota Roja, 'The Red Press,' in Mexico.
In Arab countries, nightly news wouldn't hesitate to run
the uncensored footage, but it'd be misinterpreted
as posthumous protest art—it should be shown
statistically that protest art is largely ineffective.

You've heard of the self-immolating monk
from sixty years ago. Have you heard of
the hundreds who've done the same since?
Now a corpse swung around on
a bungee cord, you'd remember!

PROP COMEDIAN

Pope.L crawling in the street
in a Superman suit
for 22 miles over 9 years

or MPA holding a plaster cast sculpture of
her father's fist in the sunlight
during gallery hours

or the hairy, naked, upside-down Austrians of Gelitin
sticking lit candles
in their assholes—

to God,
is the same as

the Israeli soldier parading around
in the red lingerie he found
in a bombed house in Gaza.

To God, the new Nakba is
a watermelon smashed with a sledgehammer
in Her schlocky comedy act.

PYNCHON

Politics is the entertainment division
of the Military-Industrial Complex.
—FRANK ZAPPA

Every TV show I watch
is about the yin and yang.
Democrats and Republicans,
Palestinians and Israelis,
rich and poor, like flies rubbing
their hands back and forth.
Friction powers the heat engine.
Where to? Pynchon knew.
From entropy to a zero state.
Everyone murder-suiciding
into no one.

STREET CATS

In the last minute of my last therapy session,
I lobbed in that not having children
is a kind of slow suicide.

That's why people have kids, I said,
they love themselves when they should
hate themselves. But this was progress:

I used to think people who have children
are like street cats, animals of the lowest order,
appreciative of the dust on blinds.

Truly, we are dust.

FOR YARA FLOWERS

Maybe I'd been spared. I might've been a spiteful mother,
the kind to let him squirm in his shit a few extra seconds
before cleaning him up, knowing he'd never remember.
But I wouldn't have. I'd have been a slavish mother,

deftly hiding my resentments, allowing them to
accumulate like a patina in a house filled with wailing
and gentle music, giggles and wet farts, the sounds
I never wanted and felt like an imposter to now miss.

I never placed flowers at the grave. It struck me as grotesque
to tear flowers from the ground where they grew,
severing their stems and shoving them in water
like formaldehyde for a corpse at a multi-day viewing.

But filing my nails, watching the spirals of dust
swirl in the sunray filled me with a selfish desire,
and I figured florists would sell flowers even if
I boycotted them, so might as well buy.

I snipped the bottoms of the stems at an angle,
refreshed their water. They were ears
strung on a soldier's necklace, heirloom tomatoes
and fresh greens on a porcelain plate. I was one

of the dum-dums. Then the signs of death appeared.
One day I up and stopped killing insects, bothering
instead to trap them in a glass and deposit them outside,
a measured heroic euphoria fizzing in my chest.

Even lights left on in empty rooms troubled me.
I knew I was taking it too far. When I switched the light
above my kitchen sink off at the end of the night,
I thought, You can rest now, or You can rest now, sweetie,

feeling affection for the wires holding the electrical charge,
the delicate searing glass, the fragile filament absorbing
the hot glow. I personified it as a child might.

SEPTUM

When my IUD's seven-year lifespan was up,
I felt better after the foreign object was out.
The hijabi receptionist at Planned Parenthood
cornered me to ask how I care for my curly hair,

volunteering that her second child would be her last
because her five-day-long labor had culminated in
a heart attack. It's not like I wanted to get pregnant,
I just wanted to be unencumbered by precautions.

It was like my deviated septum, there was no reason
not to get the surgery, I just didn't want to.
Besides which, the doctor wouldn't promise
not to change the shape of my nose.

I still don't have an IUD and I could have
an accident anytime. And I can't think of IUDs
without thinking of IEDs, even all these years
after America's destruction of Iraq.

TOLD YOU OBAMA WOULDN'T CLOSE GUANTANAMO

I'm the son of a factory worker
who was the son of a farmer
but they made me drink
blood. I don't know whose.

They cut a Star of David
into my forehead
with a boxcutter.

My blood filled my eyes.
The salt of it stung.
My eyelashes clotted.

They penetrated a German
Shepherd and then me.
The animal howled and died.
I died. The first time

they brought water
and towels, I thought
it was to clean me.

DUNK TANK

Death is sitting
on the whoopie cushion.

Your face smashed
in the birthday cake.

The seat collapses,
you fall into the dunk tank.

A bombardment of laughter,
and you bask in it.

KALTHOUM

The sound of Om
fills the emptiness,

the Arabic word
for mother.

HI, MOM!

Might be your first words
after your last words

and the feeling that greets you
when you die.

TCHOTCHKE

The chrome Ganesh I bought at Burlington Coat Factory
sits on a shelf reflecting sunlight a decade after I plucked it
from a messy clearance bin with my cousin who'd been
in the country only a few days. She needed a winter coat
and I wanted a totem to taunt her that her efforts had failed—

in the old country, she'd carted me around to priests to treat
what she'd diagnosed as anger at God for my mother's death.
It was part of our push pull man woman atheist theist English
Arabic American Palestinian slut virgin first cousin thing.
She lives in San Antonio now. Yesterday she texted me.

She's in town and wants me to meet her children. I'd long
been proud of my defiance, my choice not to have kids,
but my pride now had a curdled layer of shame, the way—
in the decade since I bought the gaudy elephant still glinting
in my eyes—my atheism has congealed into a kind of belief.

OSIRIS

The men who chopped up Osama bin Laden's body
and scattered his parts in the ocean
were too stupid to know about the myth
they were enacting. They laid tarp
like mobsters and distributed electric hand saws
as if to family members carving
a prize turkey.

                                        Death is a prize
in my dreams, the waking I win after
terror. Sometimes when I'm falling asleep,
I imagine myself wrapped like a mummy
and thrown overboard, weighted to sink
through the darkness to the total blackness
of the ocean floor, my testicles put on ice
and sent to my wife. Blind wormy fish,

eels and gelatinous creatures slither at the bottom
of the ocean, sensing their way across the cold,
silken floor, roving for something to nibble,
moving to the next thing and the next
until they come to me
and struggle, giving up, unable
to chew through my sealed tight,
perfect wrapping.

KSM

I wake up every hour or two, sometimes three.
I dream it's fire they pour in my lungs and throat.
Sometimes it's smoke that chokes and seizes me.
Usually it's fire. This confirms for me it's Shaytan,
the Americans with oxblood eyes.

They put a clock on my life and broke the clock.
Time isn't like time. The hours screech by but
I swear I'm not depressed. This is my reward.
The worse they treat me, the more I know
I scored against Shaytan. Their souls are like
Kleenexes they spit into. Written on the tissues,
the names of their daughters and sons.

They think they are breaking my mind,
but Allah loves me more the more they try.
My mind is a boulder glowing with Allah's light.
But Shaytan taught me this stupid game where
a rock crushes a knife, but paper flattens a rock.

SAINT GEORGE KILLING THE DRAGON

The dragon was in her late seventies.
She got up to her tits in quicksand
and asked her trapper, *This is what you do*
with your time? Plot subterfuge with misogynists?

He tattooed the bottom of her feet,
clipped her ear and tagged it
with a numbered ribbon.

She had a bazooka in her throat
but he speared her,
pushing it through like a catheter
till her toes were blue figs.

Much later,
a boy seeing a plate of this murder
hanging in his uncle's living room

clapped his hands furiously
at different spots in the air,
trying to kill a flea.

FASTING FOR GAZA

Moved by an activist leader,
I fasted for Gaza
for two and a half days.

Afterward, I ate less than usual,
but a week later reverted to
normal portions at regular intervals.

This has happened a few other times,
pathetic attempts to deprive myself
in solidarity with hunger in the news.

Jenny Craig should advertise with Al Jazeera.

GO LEFT

The trees in my poems are not
the trees in Richard Powers's novel.
Maybe that doesn't mean anything to you.
I haven't even finished his book.

You're probably thinking my trees
are powerless victims. I'm Palestinian
after all. How can I compete with
Richard Powers's knowing, wondrous trees
plus your biases?

Months ago, I unfurled the wrapper
of a Dove chocolate that read, *When life*
isn't going right, go left, which tempted me

to scrap a short story told in the voice
of the hospital aide who is cleaning the room
where hunger striker Khader Adnan has just died—

and instead write a story about
a Palestinian cannibal.

But then Israel committed genocide
and I couldn't write anything at all.
I'm editing this poem on the 100th day.
I refuse to read *The New York Times*

but I confess, I opened the link
my sister sent me to watch

the magnified video of
a small, mouth-like opening

through which plants breathe and also
apparently scream when lacking sun
or water, or when a limb is hacked off.

Richard Powers says trees whisper
to each other; they cry out
in danger and pain.

Why is it beautiful
that more suffering
has been added to the world?

PROMISE OF THE FUTURE

I was a futurist,
imagining utopian life ahead.
Now here I am, halfway dead.

I thought scientists could defeat death.
Yet here I am, ripping bread with my teeth.
In forty years, we won't need teeth.

I'll be eighty then, close to death.
I'll hate what evades me then
as I hate it now.

KNOWLEDGE AND LIBERATION

Visual artists know more than
musicians.

Writers know more than
visual artists.

Philosophers know more than
writers.

Quantum physicists know more than
philosophers.

Vedantists know more than
quantum physicists.

Vedantists know
nothing.

FULLNESS

Behind eternity isn't
more eternity. Nothing
lies in wait. Maybe you

think of it as a vacuum,
a void at the center of
the universe, a dot

that went all ways
at once, an asterisk,
footnote to everything.

Nothing is the Godhead
that gobbles the world
in one fell swoop,

but has no anus.

KALPAS

A kalpa is a single breath
expanding a speck into the cosmos,
contracting the cosmos down to a speck,

into the cosmos, down to a speck,
into the cosmos, down to a speck,
into the cosmos, down to a speck,

This breath in here and that sun up there
are exactly the same.

—Chandogya Upanishad

HYPNIC JERK

You dream you're falling

to your death. Your body
jerks, you're scared awake.

This happens night after
night. Aeon after aeon,

Big Bangs blow up,
thumb on a detonator:

Nothing—All—
Nothing—All—

Curving back upon My own Nature,
I create again and again.

—Bhagavad Gita

MAO

In the morning while I slurped black coffee,
I took three screenshots in quick succession—
bang bang bang, like pulling a trigger.

The video started on a dirty floor, a man saying
Bismillah al-Rahman al-Rahim under his breath as
the camera panned to a room of four Gazan men

shot dead by the Israelis. Velour blankets
under each one, murdered in their beds.
Four of ~~forty~~ four hundred thousand.

I went about my day. Later that night,
I watched the new *Mr. & Mrs. Smith*.
Donald Glover talked shit about Detroit

so that was cool. I coveted a Noguchi
pendant. My dog slept across my legs,
her velvety ears flopping in dream.

I doodled a Mr. Potato Head face
in the margin of my notebook. It sort of
looked like Mao. Why do I suddenly

want this Mao tattooed, I don't care
where, on my arm, over my heart by
the ١٩٤٨ obscured by my chest hair?

My mother would hate me for saying this,
but there was something Mao-like about her
face in the open casket.

It looked like a birthday cake,
mushy and cold. Embalming
in the 90s wasn't as good as it is now.

She looked like a cake-faced Mao
as I leaned over the glossy wood to kiss her.
I slept under her maroon velour

blanket for years, till my Jewish girlfriend
made fun of it, but by then we'd fucked on it
for a month and honestly, I'd forgotten it

had ever belonged to my mother. It was just
a blanket I'd had for a really long time.
I got rid of it because I liked the girl

and wanted her to think I was cool.
Shoved it in some Chicago dumpster.
Don't even have a picture of it.

TIGER'S NEST MONASTERY

I shot blow darts at a man's back.
Slow streaks of blood caressed
the pale curve of his ass.

He had swirled scars on his thighs,
carved like *Spiral Jetty*.
My French assistant spat on them.
I had him kneel and we spat on his face.

We invited over a muscled sadist
we hadn't vetted. He arrived
drunk, swigging brown liquor
from a water bottle that crackled
in his mouth.

I argued with him to leave
and he knocked me out.
When I came to, the masochist
had pulled a knife on the sadist
and was calmly giving him
one last chance to go.

Later, a little choked up,
I called the sadist and made my own threats,
saying my jaw was broken—it wasn't—
and that I had no insurance—I did.
He apologized and gave me his address
where he left a check for me in his mailbox.

The masochist sent me pics
of his trip to southeast Asia.
In one, a Buddhist temple in Bhutan
is perched on the mountainside behind him,
like an elaborate blow dart.

FIGHT

Hamas is not the cartel.

Roll the window down, smell
the humid sea air, glue smeared
on cracked concrete.

If I use pliers to stretch your nipples
past the Apartheid Wall to Cairo
or the thunder behind the darkened
sunset, should I expect you'd propose
we hug, chest to chest?

NOSE KISS

In the math problem where heaven is
everything and hell is nothing and God
is the highest form of society,
a society of one can be solved as:

Heaven is the same everything
nothing is like hell is the same
nothing everything is, the way
infinity verges toward zero.

JACUZZI

We used to live in trees,
before that we were fish.
We were a brew of crap
in the jacuzzi of the oceans.

How far we may yet evolve,
until God is a mother with
eyeshadow like a whore,
the stars her glitter.

BARBECUE

250,000 years after
the discovery of fire,
we still ate raw meat.
But good things come
to those who wait.

It took us a quarter
of a million years
to arrive at barbecue,
so give God a little
more time.

INFINITY IS JUST ANOTHER PLACE

Our babies will grow up
and marry each other.
Their babies will marry
each other, too.

Eventually, no one will
be alone. Babies won't
resemble babies so much
as the wings of flies

flapping and swooping
so fast, God will clap
her hands. Each clap
is a Big Bang.

In the spacelessness
of her touching hands,
freeze frame applause
looks like prayer.

My wife's therapist
told her everything we do
is a prayer—nothing
becomes everything,

energy becomes matter.
The hourglass is flipped
again. God applauds
nothing.

PIGEONS

I dreamt I was picking the cancer
out of my mother's lungs like hornets
from a nest, tossing the scraps to the side
as if to a dog. I woke parched, the house
miserably hot. The AC had cut out.

I checked the thermostat, groggily jabbing
the buttons, prying at the plastic cover
until it creaked and snapped open.
I replaced the batteries,
expecting a hush of cool air,
but the air didn't move.

My mind went to tampering,
petty psychological warfare.
I suspected they kept tabs on me,
recording me from a distance. I felt it.
They knew how much money I had,
who I emailed and texted, where I went.
That's what they got off on.

I opened all the windows,
changed into a tank top and shorts.
A cloud shoved off and sunlight
blanketed my face, forcing me to
close my eyes.

I felt exposed, even if no one could see
me from a distance, even if the birds

didn't register my nakedness—
as long as the birds weren't drones.
I ran my hands over my genitals
to make sure they were real.

Whenever I came face to face with
soldiers at checkpoints or in Jerusalem,
they were part of the scenery, like pigeons
perched at the top of the soot-streaked
Damascus Gate, buried under
fatigues in the heat, tortoise backs
strapped to their heads.

In the kitchen where the windows
faced the oldest houses of the village,
I drank gritty guava juice from a mottled
bottle. In the living room
I stood at the glass door facing the olive
trees, the wide settlement behind them.
I couldn't see anyone who could see me.

THE SUN'S SILENCE

Is a lie. I handed God a jar of my bowels
in a dream and woke with a sentence
I don't remember the source of—
Nameless light makes us one.
I suppose I believed
the feeling it gave me. It was like how
nothing can live on the sun, but the sun lives.

YOGI

It's ironic that atheists and theists are both
right: there is nothing *and* there is God.
They're not the same, but they are one.

To say it a bit like Yogi Berra,
there's one in none.

MILIEU

The very moment God falls asleep,
i.e. dies, the material world is created
in an explosion that expands until God
wakes again, i.e. the immaterial world
is recreated. But eventually, one gets
antsy meditating. God is like that
extremely wealthy type who has it all
but is unhappy, i.e. a rich douchebag.

AT THE ARAB AMERICAN NATIONAL MUSEUM

In the dark auditorium, the spotlight
comes down on the oud player
seated center stage. He plays
an unaccompanied, structureless melody,

then holds a pregnant note
until the stage bursts with light.
The full orchestra breaks in all together

and my father looks at me, eyebrows raised,
completely overjoyed. This is the feeling

my meditation practice
would numb.

L'ORIGINE DU MONDE

Surprise myself every time I begin
a new poem without Palestine,

though nothing is my other obsession,
but that's only surprising if

you don't conceive of nothingness
as a sort of prolapsed anus (as I do),

the universe as a gaping hole
that inverts. Palestine becomes

Israel. Israel becomes nothing.
Everything comes full circle.

Nothing is what's inside the circle.
It isn't the vast, gaseous blackness

of outer space, it's the angry pink
of your insides.

LANDING IN ISRAEL

The sunset bleeds orange-red through the windows.
As the plane descends, a hundred Orthodox Jews sing
Israel's national anthem in rousing Hebrew.
When the plane touches down, brakes roaring
over the hundred voices singing
and the swell of cheers and applause,
I can't help but to be swept up in their emotion,
smiling and unsmiling, smiling and unsmiling.

INSIDE THE DOME OF THE ROCK

Under the archway of al-Mawazin,
a boy sold fuzzy olives from a silver bowl.

Tiered chandeliers hung in concentric circles,
unafraid pigeons bobbled at my feet and
perched high on ornately patterned walls,
clunky fans pushed the warm air around.

A few steps led down to a room that held
a section of sacred rock that I approached
sanctimoniously. There was an eerie coolness
to the air. I was starting to get the heebie-jeebies.

I imagined it lifting off like an alien spaceship
that shot through outer space up into heaven
carrying the Prophet Mohammed, PBUH,
like the cowboy riding a nuclear warhead

in *Dr. Strangelove*, or Aladdin on his flying
carpet, or Hanuman, the green half-monkey,
half-man trickster god who lifted a mountain
and flew it to Rama to save his brother's life.

What mountain can be lifted
to stop the genocide? What green man
will lift it? What carpet will carry the
four hundred thousand Israel killed
to the New Jerusalem?

CHAPLIN

When the captain braced us for coarse clouds,
I used a straw broom to paint *Ceasefire*
in dripping green block letters
on the plane's olive wood exit door.

It thrust open and my eyes dried
as I was sucked into the assaulting sky.
I maneuvered the broom between my legs,
a teetering sensation in my groin,

hurtling toward the Spanish Garden
in Jericho where I met my parents
and we walked together to the town square
making meaningless conversation.

A thick crowd was gathered like
flies trapped in a honeyed plastic bag
in the greenish afternoon, sitting atop
car hoods and squatting on the curb,

leaning on concrete flower pots,
against storefronts and each other's shoulders,
hundreds huddled in the manara,
laughing at the Charlie Chaplin movie
projected on the outdoor screen—

my laughter, masked by the crowd's,
unhinged and uncontrollable,

my stomach seizing, feeling I may
choke, my eyes sore, bleary with tears
at the life I never lived.

DETERMINISM

I dream I'm soaring
Above a highway
Like a human balloon
Coasting in the wind
And I have to fart
But if I fart
I'll fall to the pavement and die
I'll die if I touch anything at all
If the wind sails me into a building
I'll die
If I brush against swaying powerlines
I'll die
If a common bird boops me
I'll die
And though I am deeply sad
I hold in my urgent fart
Till my leg muscles shake
And my heart palpitates
I look at the passing scenery
A gray river cutting through flat fields
Offshoot shopping plaza cities
I'm like a lone astronaut
Adrift in daylit space
Running out of oxygen
Till I can't hold it in my body any longer
So I take a big last breath
And I let it all out
And while running out of time was terrifying
Death is a huge relief

THE ANIMAL

Death is almost as humiliating
as going through Ben Gurion Airport.
The pleasures of return are worth it, though.

WHEN I DIED

I imploded into a paramecium. I slithered
to a place where I was with other Jains,
sun lovers, and hedonists, people who kneel
to place a lei around the neck of an ant,
get stuck in half-hour orgasms like pigs'.
Sex with the earth was smiled upon, despite
harm to plant life. When I closed my eyes,
I saw the names of God twisting in the soil.
Everyone got their own Dome of the Rock.

SPECIES DYSPHORIA

I give interviews about my death
on first dates.

I don't die,
I just eat a lot of salad.

I hand my dog a pig's ear
and realize I'm a survivor.

The news makes no sense to me
because I can't smell the people.

I clear my throat till the neighbors,
fed up, move out.

Out of all the isms,
jism is my favorite.

I'm wispy
like a watery alien,

a breatharian
eating the light of the sun.

I risk my life
changing a light bulb.

I part my hair
with a mini trampoline.

I could break my neck with
how vigorously I wash my beard.

My blood is
a stack of poker chips.

I stick a thumbtack in my belly button,
committing a little harakiri

and book a flight to Denmark
for a ride on the Euthanasia Roller Coaster—

in the ski lift to the sky burial,
my spinal cord flailing in the air like a lasso,

I come face to face with my
encumbrance, the expansive me.

WHAT A LIGHT

Here I am dying
Somewhere back there
My heart stopped thumping
All I'm thinking
My family, my job, all of earth
Fuck em

Little glowy sugar cube
Floating toward me
Whisking me away

THE FLEA

Tried killing a flea
against my sweater,
but just pushed it into the fluff.

When I removed my hand,
it calmly skittered away
in humpy little zigzags.

The whole world's empty.
It doesn't matter
what we do to each other.

MY AERODYNAMICS

As I fell from the sky, I smelled fish.
The fish was in my mouth.
My eyes were fish eyes, bulging, bugged out.

I fell like this for years,
in the fishy air. I stopped panicking.
I could think as I fell.

I missed spaghetti.
I was a model, hair blown back
in the wind. I was thirty-five.

I was fifty-three. The sun
winked at me like bar light
through a shot of whisky.

Nights were easier. I actually
fell, harhar, asleep. Five minutes
here, ten minutes there.

Open sky, open darkness.
I drank. I pissed myself.
I stripped my clothes off in the sky.

I was very cold. I hugged myself
and it changed my aerodynamics.
I began spinning out of control.

I vomited clear rain.
I refused water.
Refused breath.

I missed my daughter.
I missed my wife. I missed our home.
I missed smoking. I accepted

I'd never leave this blue prison.
How quickly my mind adjusted,
but I was dangerously bored.

AFTER CAMÕES

A lot of people don't
exist. It's funny, you

popping up like this.
There's so much water

in your eye. Thanks
for stopping by.

FINAL MONTAGE

Calm emanated from the old swami I met.
His B.O. did, too.

The Fourth Noble Truth: a misnomer, a cheap trick.
It's an Eight-Fold Path!

Cute thought bubbles up, a floppy water balloon,
chuck it at your head.

I lost all my friends; my life ended suddenly.
I should celebrate!

Dying's not so bad, though it can be a long slog—
living's often worse.

A hologram Christ I bought in Jerusalem—
eyes open, eyes shut.

God's a bad movie; at the end of the drama,
it was just a dream.

My widowed father, I saw him cry only once,
watching *Patch Adams*.

Star child's fetal curl; planet's cooing and burbling,
puking and shitting.

The Dome of the Rock, royal blue and gleaming gold.
Pigeons run inside.

Sunny balcony. Bee falls in my orange juice,
flails, swims in circles.

I crush half its legs—the centipede jolts to life,
dancing, speaking tongues.

I lord over bugs. I trap a fly in a jar
of crushed tomatoes.

Lashes camouflage, at the brim of an eyelid,
a perched mosquito.

Unseen teen sniper high in the checkpoint tower.
A nerve-racking walk.

Two homeless brothers, their mother under rubble
behind where we talk.

As a kid at night, pretending to die alone,
playing war in bed.

Ramzi or Nadeem, names I wanted then.
More Arab than mine.

Coked-up Parisian in the David Lynch nightclub
calls me sand______.

Short hike from my house to Mahmoud Darwish's grave,
a pack of wild dogs.

Throwing pillows high over the Apartheid Wall,
not all go over.

Some poems, don't remember writing them.
Some old lovers, too.

I pocket a rock, my red rock from my red soil.
I may not return.

NOTES

The Palestinian Chair

"God said (and already / you can tell I'm making this up)" is taken from Tony Hoagland's poem "Marriage Song" in *Priest Turned Therapist Treats Fear of God*. The second stanza includes text from the book *Consequence* by former Abu Ghraib interrogator Eric Fair. The Palestinian Chair was a torture device used by US army interrogators on Iraqi detainees in Fallujah, after learning the technique during joint training exercises with the Israeli military. The Israelis presumably called it the Palestinian Chair because they were torturing Palestinians in it.

Aaron Bushnell Malachi Ritscher Mohamed Bouazizi

Tarek el-Tayeb Mohamed Bouazizi (1984-2011) was a 26-year-old fruit vendor who set himself on fire on December 17, 2010 in Sidi Bouzid, Tunisia, an act which became a catalyst for the Tunisian Revolution and the wider Arab Spring.

Malachi Ritscher (1954-2006) was a fixture in Chicago's experimental jazz scene who killed himself on November 3, 2006 via self-immolation to protest the US war on Iraq.

Aaron Bushnell was a 25-year-old active-duty US Air Force member who self-immolated in front of the Israeli embassy in DC on February 25, 2024, to protest the genocide in Gaza. He live-streamed his protest, stating: "I will no longer be complicit in genocide. I am about to engage in an extreme act of protest, but compared to what people have been experiencing in Palestine at the hands of their colonizers, it's not extreme at all. This is what our ruling class has decided will be normal." His last words as he burned in protest were "Free Palestine."

Kalpas

In Buddhist cosmology, kalpas are unfathomably long periods of time. Longer than the time it would take to fill a huge empty cube that is sixteen miles wide and sixteen miles high if, once every hundred years, you insert a tiny mustard seed into the cube. At the rate of one mustard seed every hundred years, the huge cube will be filled even before the kalpa ends. Longer than it would take, at the same once-a-century frequency, for the brushing of a small piece of silk once every hundred years against a mountain, 16-x-16-x-16 miles large, to wear that mountain away. According to the Buddha, the mountain will be completely depleted even before the kalpa ends.

"Kalpas" Lion's Roar: Buddhist Wisdom for Our Time, December 14, 2016

ACKNOWLEDGMENTS

I am grateful to the editors of the following magazines for first publishing these poems:

The Paris Review: "My Aerodynamics"
The Drift: "Elsewhere"
The Georgia Review: "Tchotchke"
The Adroit Journal: "Bleeding Tree"
Under a Warm Green Linden: "Secret"
Hunger Mountain: "Final Montage"
The Margins: "Chaplin"
The Rumpus: "Septum"
Iterant: "For Yara Flowers"
Paperbag: "Species Dysphoria," "Buddha's Bad Meal," "Clit,"
"Misandry," "Eat Cunt for Mental Health"
mercury firs: "Fullness," "When I Died," "Fight"
Poetry Daily: "Fullness" (reprint)
Foglifter: "Ode to _________ _________"
Adi Magazine: "The Palestinian Chair"
Honey Literary: "Osiris"
Sampsonia Way: "Promise of the Future"

Infinite thanks to Lindsey Boldt. Ham with a side of ham!

And to Stephen Motika; the dream team at Nightboat; Carol, Susan, Sadie, Brin, and most of all, Laura.

Edward Salem is the author of *Intifadas* (2026), the winner of the Kathryn A. Morton Prize in Poetry. His writing has appeared in *The Paris Review*, *The Yale Review*, *Granta*, *The New York Review of Books*, *Poetry*, and numerous other venues.

NIGHTBOAT BOOKS

Nightboat Books, a nonprofit organization, seeks to develop audiences for writers whose work resists convention and transcends boundaries. We publish books rich with poignancy, intelligence, and risk. Please visit nightboat.org to learn about our titles and how you can support our future publications.

The following individuals have supported the publication of this book. We thank them for their generosity and commitment to the mission of Nightboat Books:

Kazim Ali • Anonymous (4) • Ava Aviva Avnisan • Jean C. Ballantyne • Will Blythe • Rob Byrnes • V. Shannon Clyne • Theodore Cornwell • Gisela Gamper • Photios Giovanis • Amanda Greenberger • David Groff • Daniel Handler • Sarah Heller • Karen Holtzman • Parag Rajendra Khandhar • Katy Lederer • Shari Leinwand • Daniel Levine • Elizabeth Madans • Ricardo Maldonado • Pooja Mehta • Ethan Mitchell • Claudia Morgan • Caren Motika • Elizabeth Motika • Asker Saeed • The Leslie Scalapino - O Books Fund • Amy Scholder • Thomas Shardlow • Eric Suchyta • Benjamin Taylor • Mohan Trivedi • Jerrie Whitfield & Richard Motika • Clay Williams

This book is made possible, in part, by grants from the New York City Department of Cultural Affairs in partnership with the City Council and the New York State Council on the Arts Literature Program.

Everything is just nothing repeating itself.

—GEORGE HERRIMAN